FOOTPRINTS
IN THE
MIST

FOOTPRINTS
IN THE
MIST
A PALESTINIAN SOUL

FARID S. BITAR

iUniverse, Inc.
Bloomington

Footprints in the Mist
A Palestinian soul

iUniverse books may be ordered through booksellers or by contacting:

iUniverse
1663 Liberty Drive
Bloomington, IN 47403
www.iuniverse.com
1-800-Authors (1-800-288-4677)

Because of the dynamic nature of the Internet, any web addresses or links contained in this book may have changed since publication and may no longer be valid. The views expressed in this work are solely those of the author and do not necessarily reflect the views of the publisher, and the publisher hereby disclaims any responsibility for them.

Any people depicted in stock imagery provided by Thinkstock are models, and such images are being used for illustrative purposes only.
Certain stock imagery © Thinkstock.

ISBN: 978-1-4620-4032-2 (sc)
ISBN: 978-1-4620-4033-9 (ebk)

Printed in the United States of America

iUniverse rev. date: 08/08/2011

DEDICATION

In memory of Laila & Saleem and all Palestinian souls...

CONTENTS

FOOTPRINTS IN THE MIST, A PALESTINIAN SOUL...

The plight of Palestine has haunted me since childhood; I was six years old, living with my family in Jericho, in the valley of Jordan, when the 1967 six day war erupted.

I lost my grandmother, uncle, aunt and cousin Sa'id in the bloodshed that engulfed our home. This was more than forty years ago, but I remember it like yesterday.

The Palestinian struggle for self determination-statehood has continued in all the years between those yesterdays still become my todays. In over half a century of conflict-1948-1953-1967-1982, the first intifada from '88-'92, and the second intifada raging since '99, including the latest invasion by the Israeli army into Gaza Dec. 27th-2008, which lasted 21 days and left more than 1500 civilians perished. It seems neither side has yet learned that peace will never come at the end of a gun.

"Conspiracy-Confliction-Deterioration-Annihilation-Refugees in the millions... War crimes, chemical weapons, children dead in the hundreds..."

When I was in my twenties, an ex-patriot Palestinian finding my way in New York City,

(I returned to my Jerusalem, where my family still resides and other parts of the West Bank and Gaza, with the intention of settling there), and after graduating from Baruch College-CUNY with a Finance degree, I landed a job with a law firm in 1983, I enjoyed success until I was suddenly and unjustly fired by my boss who called me a "sand nigger". It was the time when Israel invaded Lebanon to get rid of the PLO, his secretary had placed an article on my desk from the " New York Times" with a short note, stating that my people are murderers, she gave my boss an ultimatum, it's her, who's been working there for 20 years or me. I left her the next day another article from the same newspaper, with a note, and look what your people do in Lebanon, bulldozing and killing Palestinian civilians. I was told to go back to my "murdering people, the plane hi-jackers".

Though he did not see things the same way, he was actually and figuratively a Semite cousin of mine, inasmuch as "our people" in biblical Canaan. The memory of that bitter and deeply ironic incident inspired me to write an angry poem "Sand Niggah".

I also went through many incidents when I was attending Baruch College, I was accused of being dangerous due to my Palestinian background, and I had two of my grades lowered by ignorant Professors. Again I felt very hurt and insulted at the same time. I started experiencing racial profiling at a young age. It had left resentful imprints on my growing up in America. It gave me a push to write many poems describing the experiences that I went through. I also chronicled the events that I witnessed the pain and misery of the armed conflict of the first intifada. I felt torn between the war stricken place of my roots and the relative peace and ease of life in NYC.

In 1996, I edited-translated-transliterated a book of poetry "Treasury of Arabic Love",
From the Jahiliah time of the Arab poets to the present day, it's a book about love and beauty, to show that Arabs have a rich culture.

In 2007, I produced a CD-Fatoosh, In Arabic; Fatoosh derives from a root word meaning 'to search'. These poems are set to music which represents my own search for meaning in madness; they are a humble offering and personal plea for peace to my Palestinian people and my cousins, the Israelis and to people of goodwill everywhere to help find a better way.

All migrating birds, even a dove that circles the globe in Diaspora carrying an olive branch in its beak, needs a place to roost. I dedicate this book to the over five million Palestinian refugees living in exile in some 26 countries through out the world, without the right of return and to every victim that has fallen in Lebanon, Iraq, Afghanistan, Darfur-Sudan, Rwanda, Armenia and all other genocides past and present. The hatred and violence must STOP.

AL SHUTAT (THE DISPLACEMENT)

Disaster   dispersement   dismemberment
Displaced but never discarded.
Passing old streets, destroyed houses,
I look for faces from long ago—
Where has everyone gone?
Another day lapses,
and another and another;
ghosts dwell in the destroyed
villages of '48.
Exiled all my life, I will return one day
to the garden of my house to see
the Dome of the Rock from my rooftop;
talk to my neighbor, visit the Indian Hospice,
my family's compound,
relive memories of the Napalm bombs
that blanketed the place
and burned and killed my family.

I remember water lilies,
the fig and lemon tree.
I once knocked on a door in Al-Qatam'un.
A lady answered and shouted,
What do you want!
I replied, *To see my father's house.*
She slammed the door in my face,
It must be another country you're looking for.
I begged her to let me in, screaming,
This is my father's house—I am holding the deed to it!
I passed by the ruins of Hebron's Gate
where my father's shop once was.
And where the wall of Jerusalem once stood
has now become No Man's Land.

Why should Auschwitz and Dachau
be repeated in Gaza and Jenin?
In Deir Yasin and the Khisa'as villages of '47?
Why the Haganah's ethnic cleansing
on the northern coast of Palestine?
Expulsions, attacks on local villages?

One day we Palestinians will return
to al-Barweh, Qatam'un,
Deir Yasin and the Khisa'as villages of '48.
Rachel Corrie will be re-born.
My voice will keep circling the skies
so the conscience of the world will hear.
Darwish and Kanafani will resurrect.
The children will not have to starve in Gaza.

No more ethnic cleansing!
No more Balfour Declarations!
No more empty U.N. resolutions!
No more mass killings of a civilian population!
Simply no more!

I am asking for justice.
I am asking for dignity.
I am asking for my home back.

Remember us.
Keep praying for us.

TO MY JERUSALEM

City of my birth, my memories of you
are both pleasant and painful.
I still run in the narrow streets of the Old City
along walls centuries old, built by
Salah al-Din, vanquisher of the Crusaders.

I walk the Via Dolorosa, in the footsteps of Jesus.
I enter the Dome of the Rock,
where Muhammad ascended to the seven skies.
I still follow in my father's footsteps
as he heads for his shop—
narrow alleys, streets, and entrances,
the smell of jasmine and honeysuckle,
souqs, souvenir shops, and countless markets:
the spice market, the copper market,
meat market, sweets market . . .
Faces seen day in day out
in the tiny hummus and falafel cafes,
the family butcher carving our favorite
cuts of meat for Eid . . .
Memories of me running to the market
for my mother's missing ingredients,
the smell of fresh coffee,
the coal burner in winter,
barbeque in spring,
and images of my mother
tending plants in the garden,
visiting the holy places—Omar's Mosque,
The holy Sepulcher,
stores, houses, bakeries . . .

I remember well the air raid sirens, too,
October's War, 1973—The Yom Kippur War,
fighter jets thundering in the sky, bombs exploding
as my brother and I run to safety.
The look of fear on my mother's face,
the blackened windows, shuttered shops during curfew time.
I remember the anger of the Zionist enemy after the war.
I remember the demonstrations against the occupation.
I remember the fallen victims resisting the occupier.
I remember the happiness of the nation as the enemy was losing.

Then I remember better days,
when I played marbles in the dirt.
When I walked to school every day,
bought a shawarma sandwich
and drank 7-Up with my mother.

My beloved Jerusalem,
You live in my soul.
You live in my dreams.

TO AN IGNORANT WORLD

Running on empty streets
   I send my dreams to the *corazones*
   I converse with myself
   I drift away
   I run once more

I see my Semite cousin running as well
   Carrying a brief case
   Dressed in black & white
   As usual
   Hair curled up
   Hat twirled up
   Threads falling down
   Scurrying to his golden temple

Thought he was heading to his Wailing Wall in Jerusalem
   I guess I was wrong
   I was in Newark you know

Yearning comes over me
   I send my regards to my resisting nation
   In Gaza land
   Jenin
   Ramallah

This time around
I will not read to an empty space
I will inform this ignorant world
About suffering, resistance and martyrdom
   I will be satisfied then
   I will be content then and only then

Palestine lives forever

WHERE SHOULD I LAND...?

Stranger at the door of hopefulness
Knocking, asking for forgiveness . . .
My tears soaking the bloody dead
My candle extinguished at dusk . . .

Flying over strange lands—Unknown to me
I am Fatoosh—the Flying injured bird—
Searching for HOME
Should I land on God Bless America?
The land of past massacres—Natives
Millions exterminated to make space for another

Or the land of the Euphrates
The land of being reverberated
By again the Bless you America
Or the land of New Zealand
Where East-Meets-West
And nothing much happens
Or the land of Afghanistan
Troop buildup—thank you Obama
Taliban on the rise in Wazirestan
Or the Land of Milk and Honey
My ancestors land
Those idiots that gave up my land
Or the lands of Nepal and Tibet
Once peaceful
And thanks to China-no more
I have been flying for so long
I need to land
I need you to give permission to land
So I can die peacefully
I mean land peacefully
Before being shot down
By the mighty IDF . . .

O! JERICHO

Driving downhill into the valley
Mountains so old Bedouins still dwell in it
Prophets walked through it
Abraham   Moses   Mohammad

Lowest point on earth
Where else can you go but up?
Childhood city of mine

Reached the famous Sea Level stone
Had to stop and kiss it
Eerie feeling
Ears popped from pressure
Wife couldn't hear
No more

Got to the outskirts of the city
Israeli boarder patrol
The questions started
I have been refused entry
For the past twenty-two years to be exact
Not this time   God is good
No Man's Land
Palestinian land
Salaam Allahu Aliekum (may peace be upon you)
Wa'aliekum As-salaam (and peace upon you)
Welcome home son
Guards yelled smiling
I also was smiling

Passed by the "Head Hospital"
You see I ran away from home
At age four to look for
My father who's never home
Mother said "Your father King of the Apple Market
Is at work"
I said in my head "I know where that market is"
Got hit with a chicken truck
Right in front of the hospital
They scooped me up with my
Head cracked wide open

Looked for the house
I grew up in   still there
Said hello to the balcony
The one I slept in
In the very hot summer nights
Same balcony that I saw dead people from
When the enemy raped my sleepy town

Sipped mint tea
Jericho has the best mint tea on earth
Tasted the sweetest oranges on earth
Felt I'm back to my happy childhood
Felt I'm in *deja vu* land
When I smelled the rain
Evaporating in the hot summer days
Poof   gone in seconds
Where I walked through the streets
When I was my older brother's tail
Going to school   Terra Sancta

Jericho O! Jericho
Home of the Mount of Temptation
The Umayyad Winter Palaces
Home of the best lemon trees
Where I smelled the jasmine perfuming the streets
Also home of the Refugee Camps
Poverty and misery nowadays

Drove through the valley
Along the River Jordan
Where Jesus washed his feet
Drove to Tiberia Lake
Drove to Nazareth
Home of the famous prophet

Jericho O! Jericho
Home of the Dead Sea
Where nothing lives now
Even fish left town

RENDITION

Landed in an American Airport
Walking in a sea of travelers
Approached by security officers
"Is your name, Anwar El-Ibrahimi"?
"Yes" I replied, what is this about?
Come with us, whisked away behind closed doors
Hooded, detained & questioned
Packaged, bundled, put on a private plane
Sent back, return to sender
With escort service of-course
Thrown in a dungent, 3 by 3 hole
Stripped, shackled, tortured a lot more
Water drowning my face,
Hit, spit on, cigarette buts up my ass
"You need to confess to your crimes", they yelled

But Sir, "Who are you"
That's none of your business
But if you insist to know
We are Rendition Team
We get answers at all cost
We have unlimited access of power & money
We are anonymous
We will disavow any accusations made by you
If you survive, or your family
If they ever find you . . .

Is your real name
Mohamed Farag Ahmad Bashmilah
Held for years
No charge, no lawyer
No one knows the hell I am in
My father died while detained

My mother put in a mental asylum
Lost my wife and kids . . .

All in the name of national security!!!
My name is unknown
I lost my life
I have done nothing
Their name is Rendition
Looking for Recognition
America claims democracy
And requires accountability

Obama wants to shut down Guantanamo
After the damage is done
After so many commit suicide
After they put my name in the mud
Obama once said: "Democracy requires accountability,
And accountability requires transparency".

Human rights ignored, tortured
And severely compromised.
I am a victim in all of this
I have done nothing
I am not waiting for apologies

Rendition Team
Misguided lost individuals
I wonder how they sleep at night
CIA—Mossad—MI6
The saviors of democracy
        I THINK NOT IN A MILLION YEARS . . .

SUNSETS AT THE SHORE,

Running away from the job
From the Human—From paying bills
Three days not enough
To forget and ignore
When on the Jersey shore
To forget the complexities
Of modern technology—computer—cell etc,
Swimming anywhere I spotted water
I am a crab and seeks refuge
Stunning sunsets—breathtaking
The various colors of orange
The many different purple colors
Stretching all across the horizon
The burning orange ball of fire
Finally heading to sleep
Wondering what mattress
Will sustain the heat
Like a painting—forever memorable
Picasso or Van Gough can't replicate
Only God can create
Rays shooting into the velvet sky
Watching a mother running behind her child
Little gray birds running away from the waves
Watching a woman collecting shells
In the dark
Watching a colorful kite flying
Way up in windy Pt. Pleasant
Shopping in Ocean Grove for Tiffany lamp

Shopping for a wicker set in Avon
Could not afford my JEEP in Sea Gate
Poets are known for poverty
But their soul is always rich
Watching the high waves
Makes me want to ride the beast
The best of times are at the sandy shore
Where I really had no reason to leave

THE ENEMY CAME KNOCKING

Introduction

I was born in a holy land. I come from the land of wars, casualty of death, destruction and construction.

I live in the West. My heart is in the East. I am very confused and sad, bewildered and mad.

The Stone Intifada

The enemy came knocking at my door.
It took me a while, but when my heart stopped racing.
I opened the door, after it almost was knocked down.
I asked,

> *What do you want form me,*
> *What do you want from my family?*
> *What do you want from my nation?*

The victims, the dead are all scattered,
In the hallways, in the hospitals,
Burned in the doorways and the byways,
They are everywhere in the corners.

The enemy yelled at me,

> *SHUT THE HELL UP!*
> *Don't utter a word.*
> *We ask the stupid questions.*
>
> *You are nothing,*
> *Your family,*
> *Your Nation is nothing . . .*

We will barge in, force into the place,
We will destroy,
We will erase the time,
We will demolish every living thing.

I said,

Why do you want destruction?
Why do you want to kill?
Why do you do what you do?

The enemy said,

Didn't I tell you to shut the hell up?

I am tired of this life, I am tired of this treatment.
The enemy wants to live, but he doesn't want me to breathe

I am a human creature and not an animal.
I am a human & not a building or a house.
I am a human being who has feelings.
I am not a plant nor an orchard to be bulldozed.

The enemy came
To crush the buildings
To crush the place
To crush my family
To crush and erase my Palestine

The place is gone, the time is lost.

The enemy came knocking at my door.

I asked my Creator, *What is the End?*
My Creator was silent, no word, no whisper, no clue.

I asked my creator for help, I heard nothing.
All is lost, all is gone.
Even my Creator is gone.

The First Intifada (1987-1992), better known "The Stone Intifada", was a civilian uprising using no heavy weapons, just stones thrown by the exhausted   Palestinian population against the world's fourth strongest army, The Israeli Defense Forces (IDF). Palestinian casualties were in the thousands, mostly civilians (men, women, and children). Their crime: resisting the occupation

CROSSING THE THRESHOLD*

A border town
Left behind
To the vultures
To the blood mongers
Crossing a Rafah town
Shaking hand with a population
Suffocating, exhausted
Walking into tattooed buildings
Of bullet hole—gas canisters
Tall Man with a 70 member clan
Spilling his guts,
full of cuts,
About his huts . . .
Huddled behind the walls
Three years to be exact
Three dead to be exact
And many times injured—exactly
Cried a little—that was me not the Man
Reached to my pocket to help the clan
Tall Man yelled "keep your money,
Just tell Netanyahu and Mubarak
lift the siege and leave me the hell alone
fix my home
To live my dream
To give my family a decent life"
White tent city-tunnels all around
Stepped in the mud
To a avoid Guevara motor man
Showing off with Motorcycle
Toured the town behind

Motorcycle young man
Told me he lost his
Mother—Brother and cousin
With tears in his eyes
Had to hug motor man
After he told me
To get the fuck out of his town
Egyptian watchman on the ground
Building a steel net to seal the border
May Allah bless the victims!
Slaughtered—bulldozed—left behind,

After allowed into Gaza for 48 hours to deliver supplies and money Jan. 1st, 2010

FLYING BIRD...

Lemon Tree
Olive Tree
Fig Tree . . .

I am transforming,
I am a shape shifter
In a leap of faith
Upside down—Life
Horizon—New
Constricted—conflicted
But committed . . .

Star formation,
In another galaxy,
Red room,
KGB,
Pino-Grigio,
Watching the waves . . .

I am,
The flying bird of Palestine.
I am,
Al-Anbar-Kandahar
Blue water surging,
Troop build-up,
And the trees blowing . . .

DEEP THROAT

give me patience and pray for me
give me a tear drop mixed with blood
give me a candle to light my ass on fire

approached deep throat at the threshold
she showed me her fangs
and proceeded to call devil miss Jones
I open the gate and stare into darkness
I close the gate and hover in resignation
what is installed for me—I keep asking

I want to vomit on this mad world
a human making ruckus and enjoying it
a human committing atrocities in the forbidden zone
deep throat smirks in the background
calling on devil Miss Jones to dwell in misery
observing a fellow man twisting in the dust

I was the one that was attacked
I will demand my honor and dignity
I have to rid of deep throat & devil miss Jones
I know that Allah is always around
a tyrant is blocking my exit and entrance
my nightmare reminds me
of SAUNDI tsunami—Japan
strongest earthquake ever recorded
erasing thousands of lives
a woman crying, her family all gone
danger can strike out of nowhere
I wish that deep throat can open her eyes

where is the justice in these crazy times
my rights have been flushed down the tubes
I know one day will come
I will claim my kingdom come
I will defeat Satan that lurks
in the woods and the work place

FLUSHED DOWN THE TUBES

New horizon coming to town
In the twilight I see a shinning light
A new millennium   a new order
A brand new empire   under the rising sun

Forget Japan the old empire under the sun
Forget the British Empire that the sun never finished setting on
Forget Stalin   Siberia   and the Gulag
An empire that stretched for 75 years
The Iron Curtain   USSR   the Hammer and the Sickle
That came crumbling down

We have a new empire under the rising sun
The empire of America and the American Army Machinery
The new high-tech precision smart bombs
Dropped from F-16s   F-17's   fighter jets
Brutality   arrogance
Bush and his cronies
Mr. Cheney   the oil man
Mr. Rumsfeld   the butcher   Popeye
Ms. Condoleezza   Olive Oil

I thought Stalin was horrible
I thought Saddam was miserable
I thought Ivan was terrible

Meet Mr. Bush   the Lynch Man
The creator of the Iraqi War   Mr. WMD
Every time new dirt is dished out about the atrocities
Of the American Army he claims he never knew

Walks like a monkey
Grins and smirks like a donkey
Keeps repeating in his head
"I can't believe I am the President of the Free World
The only super power
Hell   I can do the hell I want
and who's going to stop me now?"

The world is so lopsided
We are under the mercy of a monkey
Creator of the Guantanamo detention camp
Right on the outskirts of Fidel Castro
The last traces of Communism
You would think Castro is the Butcher of Baghdad
Think again   the American Army sends its regards

The Qur'an desecrated many times over
The Muslim world in turmoil
Newsweek claims it was flushed down the toilet
Then had to retract the story   no evidence yet

Thousands of detainees for more than three years now
No trail   no lawyers no crime to pin on
Enemy-of-the-State combatants
Thanks to Rumsfeld and the Patriot Act
"Credible evidence" the *New York Times* said

Two dead prisoners in Bagram   2002
The dirt is just coming out in 2005
Thanks to a drawing of an American soldier
Who knows what else is lurking in the walls   halls   cells

One father chained and died on the wall in a cell
Like an animal died chained on the wall
Doctor confirmed dead fly on the wall
Farmer   had a two-year-old daughter
Now fatherless   thanks to the techniques
of American Interrogation
Body buried "unknown"
Cause of death also "unknown"
Thanks to the American Army
The Savior of the Free World

Iraqi civilians   death toll in the hundreds of thousands
Iraq sinking in quick sand
Insurgency on the rise   nowhere to contain
Mus'ab al-Zarqawi bombed to smithereens
Bin Laden no where to be found
Millions of dollars offered   and nothing found

Afghanistan's death toll is never known
It must be in the thousands   if not so much more
Hundreds of caves blown to bits and no one to be found

Billions of tax dollars wasted
Iraq is getting worse and worse
My salary and yours funding the American Machinery of War
No weapons of WMD ever found
Bush said   "Saddam you have 48 hours to leave or else
We will pay you a visit"

Bush just wants the oil
And could not care less about the people of Iraq
Look at the prices at the gas pump
It's reaching the boiling point
When do we wake up and smell the roses
I never know

Cause he needs to defend the world form evil you know
And spreads democracy to the dumb Third World
He always knows more than the rest of world will ever know

A new Empire Under the Rising Sun
God bless America   I'll never know
That's one man's opinion
What do you know?

FROZEN ON THE TRACKS

In a blustery and freezing day
                the snow particles flowing in the wind

The weather is thundering and angry with the gods
                and the temperature is below sub-zero

I watch the footsteps in the innocent snow
                I watch the snow landing on the branches

I watch the snow covering everything in sight
                It covers the fields, parks, rivers, and streams

I watch the clear blue skies
                clouds passing at an alarming speed

I watch the frozen birds sitting
                quietly on the bare branches

I watch the naked trees, it's leaves
                gone with the fall

Waiting anxiously for the coming of the spring
                I am also waiting anxiously for the spring

I am tired of the constant snow
                unrelenting and unforgiving

It took me an hour to dig out my car
                I was wet all over

But I don't tire of slipping and sliding
                on the white snow

I run, I play, I fall, I laugh, and I cry
      with the innocent snow

The birds circling in the skies
      worshiping their creator

And I am still waiting, frozen
      in the very early morning on the tracks

Waiting for the Bloomfield train

BAA'OUHAA (THEY SOLD IT)

The Six Day War 1967

Conspiracy. Confliction. Deterioration. Annihilation.
Refugees in the millions.
Baa'uohaa—they sold the land

I look into the distant land;
I see the Mount of Temptation
where Jesus fasted for forty days.
I am in a very old land, Jericho,
the oldest city in the world.
Below sea level, home of the Dead Sea.
My childhood city.

Standing at the balcony,
starring, watching the enemy,
rolling down,
from the Mount of Temptation
tanks open fire

I asked my mother,
Why is the man in my house?
Not moving, not breathing—
is he sleeping?

Mother had nothing to say.
Mother, I asked,
Why is the man bleeding?
Mother, I asked, *what is the man with the army fatigue doing*
sitting at the corner, with his eyes wide open
not moving, not walking?
The next day came, and the day after and after.

He is still at the corner, not moving.
He is still starring at my balcony.
Doesn't he need to shut his eye lids?

I was six years old,
I asked all the questions,
Mother, didn't have all the answers.

I wore a blue All-Star sneaker,
It was my older brother, Mahmood's sneaker
so large it was bigger than my head.
I still wore it with pride;
it was my favorite brother's sneaker,
It was sacred to me,
I was six years old,
What the hell did I know.

I stepped on to the bus,
my family heading,
northwest bound, Jerusalem.
The whole world was moving,
eastbound to the boarder, Jordan.
The bus driver asked me,
What is this sneaker you're wearing,
and why is it so big on you?
I replied,
My favorite sneaker in the whole wide world—www.war

Baa'ouhaa

The bus driver burst out crying,
and laughing at the same time.
I stated, *Why do you cry,*
it's only my blue, All-Star sneaker,

Baa'ouhaa

BLACK SEPTEMBER, MUNICH, 1972

Finished watching "Munich", the movie of Mr. Steven Spielberg's—Hollywood style. Huge production (Malta, Paris, Athens, Beirut, etc.) portraying Palestinians as monsters and war mongers, glorifying Israel and how superior the Jewish state is, Golda Maier stating, "Shedding Jewish blood will be costly for the world from now on". A group of five so-called Unknowns with permission from Golda and the Mossad given unlimited funds to pay for information to eliminate the group of twelve that committed the massacre at the Munich Olympic games in 1972. How that list was put together is a mystery; the movie shows the human factor for the group of five, but never talks about the other side.

Mr. Spielberg omitted so many details about the Palestinian side; Golda unleashed the Air Force on the camps in Lebanon, hundreds of Palestinian civilians perished form the air raids. I guess you can watch the movie and make up your own mind. I will step in to shed some light on how, when, and why Black September was born to educate the likes of Spielberg and the rest of the world.

Al-Karameh war took place in 1968 on the Jordan River, between the PLO & Israel. The PLO retreated to Amman-Jordan; King Hussein was the ruler of the Hashemite Kingdom installed by the British Empire before 1948. In 1970, a civil war erupted between King Hussein and the PLO; a truce was declared with the intervention of Nasser, President of Egypt. Soon after, Hussein unleashed his Bedouin troops to the camps and massacred thousands of Palestinian civilians. The PLO then moved to Beirut, Lebanon. That took place in September of 1970.

Black September was created from the ashes of the dead in the camps of Amman, from the women prostituting themselves to feed their children, from hunger and poverty, from the betrayal of the Arab Regimes, from the constant killings that Israel was committing.

Israel is built on blood. Black September decided to deal blood with blood—that's the language that Israel understands. And still does nowadays in Gaza and the West Bank. The IDF just killed 121 Palestinians since last Saturday (March 1, 2008) in Gaza.

Going back to the movie, it cost Israel nearly six million dollars to eliminate the twelve members; the last one was Mohammad Salameh in 1979, the mastermind of the Munich operation, supposedly. In the interim, many civilians where killed, Palestinians and Europeans alike. They left a body of a Swiss woman, a hired-for-kill, naked, on a chair, for the world to see and learn.

The head of the Unknowns, could not finish the job—his conscience started to bother him. His wife just delivered a baby and he started getting very disturbing thoughts, became paranoid. The price you pay is not cheap.

They never show what the Palestinian side is going through. Today the average Gazan is living on a dollar a day, while the average working Israeli is living on $18,000 dollars a year. Palestinians have lost so much since the establishment of the Jewish State in '48. Palestinians had nothing to do with Hitler's Holocaust. Palestinians had nothing to do with the Diaspora of the Jews. As a matter of fact, Palestinians are dealing with their own *Shutat—al Nakbah* (Diaspora). Four million Palestinians are living all over the world, Israel's sticking point is the refusal of dealing with "The Right of Return" for the Palestinians. Every Palestinian family consists of one dead, one in jail, one in *al-Mahjar* (in exile), and one fighting for whatever is left of the land, Palestine.

I am many generations from Jerusalem, yet Israel gives me only two to three weeks to visit my home, then I have to leave. It does not give that privilege to many other millions of my people. A line from the head of the Unknowns: "You are going to rot in the camps of other countries. You will never see the time of day of your beloved land, Palestine". Peace never comes. I wonder why.

At the rate we are both going at it, it will never come, destruction is the result. Peace is out of the window.

All Israel knows is how to piss the population off, how to do vigilante-style killings of Hamas and others. Just recently, they assassinated a commander from Hezbollah, Imad Maghniyeh, to restart things with Hezbollah. Israel is still sore from the botched-up war with Hezbollah in June 2007. Israel killed hundreds of Lebanese civilians and could not finish Hezbollah. Just the other day, I read in *AM,* a New York City newspaper: "Israel is building 1,000 more houses in East Jerusalem," an occupied territory.

I ask, Why doesn't the British Empire donate some of Wales or Scotland to settle the Jews, instead of donating my Palestine, as it did in 1948. I ask, Why didn't France in the 50's, and the USA, who are now supplying weapons—napalm bombs, top-of-the-line fighter jets to finish off the Palestinian population—Why aren't they held responsible for all the genocide that Israel is committing to my nation.

Why should they not pay the price? I think they should be tried in a court of law.

The Blondie member of five stated, "I only care about Jewish blood" and kept killing. Golda said, "A good Palestinian is a *dead* Palestinian." Sharon said, "What Palestinians? They belong in Jordan; they need to move out of Judea and Samaria [the biblical names for the West Bank]." . . . father of the Jewish settlements.

I say as long as there will be a fertile Palestinian woman Israel will never rest in peace. Mr. Spielberg forgot to mention that Golda Meir stepped down from the embarrassment of the Munich dilemma; the Labor Party lost the elections and the conservative Likud, headed by Menachem Begin, struck a deal with Sadat of Egypt and signed a peace treaty in 79', that same year they assassinated the head of the Black September group, Salammah. Very ironic—land for peace, only for Egypt . . . Palestine is still in a quagmire, quicksand. Israel will never let the Palestinians live in peace . . .

BORDER PATROL—IIII

Feeling powerful
Muscling power into control
Jurisdiction—Conflict—Justification
Investigation—Interrogation

Crossing border
Border patrol
Humans feeling almighty
Blue uniform in control
God Bless America
The Land of the Free (Not Really)
Clarification—on the blue horizon

Thousand Islands—Route 81—U.S.A.
Thousand Islands—Canadian Border
How life can be nice and sweet
How life can turn sour and bleak
The luck of the draw
Life turning up or down
Felt disgusted—cheated and not so happy
To be an American

Border Patrol—God in control

BROKEN DOWN

At the Rafah crossing
Stepping into a war zone
A man sitting in a corner
Face ageless
Features unknown
I sat next to the man
Broken Down—Broken Down
Obscure objects
At the Rafah border town
A war zone left behind
Hundreds of broken down homes
Bloodied eyes
From crying over children
Destroyed lives at the Eretz crossing
Private escort into the narrow streets
Of Rafah town
Huddled in a guest house
A man spilling his guts out
About his demolished building
15 years of savings
Gone in a flash—In a flash
By the IDF soldiers
To make room for a better view
A man living in a rented house
For the third time
Sharing pictures of his
Long gone home
Israeli snipers shooting
Anything moving

Shooting fish in a barrel—Fish in a barrel
A broken down man
With tears in his eyes
Didn't know what to tell the MAN
Jobless—Homeless—and now Broken Down . . .

While visiting Rafah-Gaza Jan.2nd-2010

EYES

Mother's Day (Middle East)

Starving eyes
Singing the blues
In the early morning of the dew

Hungry empty eyes
Starring into space
In the final frontier

Desolate eyes
Calling on the dogs
Of misery

Eyes starring into emptiness
While I am swimming
In the fog of Lake Eaton

Troubled, tortured
Lamenting, disturbed
Thoughts from a bad dream

Thinking of my mother's fate
Thinking of my nation's destiny
Thinking of creatures of habits

Ma'awtinii (my homeland)
Ma'awtinii
My love for you is eternal

I will die thinking of you
I will never forsake you
I will never abandon you

SAND NIGGAH FROM PALESTINE

Said to a Semite cousin of mine,
If I'm a Sand Nigger,
then what does that make *you?*
I know I'm an Arab Semite
descendant of Ishmael—
you, my cousin the Jew,
are a Semite, too—
descendant of Yitzhak, our father is Ibrahim . . .

We're from the same race, same genes,
We both came out of the land of Canaan.
Look at me! I have olive skin and dark hair,
I have a Roman nose—so do you, my cousin,
I mean, the Sephardic one.

What—you don't recognize me?
I mean, you can't tell us apart . . .

How much do you wanna bet that I'm
a Jew or an Arab—
a dollar?
Your next paycheck?
Your seat next to me on a flight to Tel Aviv?

Appearances are deceiving . . .
Or is it the *nose* that's doing the magic?

Look at me!
Am I a Jew from the land of Isaac?
Am I Mohammed the Palestinian?
Of the two of us, which one is safe?
We are cousins, since the dawn of time . . .

And God said to Moses,
I AM WHO I AM AND WHAT I AM
AND I WILL BE WHAT I WILL BE

I must have met you in the Spanish Inquisition.
Who saved your sorry ass then
In Andalusia, Umayyad time—
who saved your sorry ass then?
In Algeria, in the Holocaust time,
When the slaughter by Hitler was taking place—
and I'm not talking about *The Sound of Music,*
the von Trapp family . . .

Didn't we make a deal in Khyber?
At the birth of Islam, when the tunnels were dug
to keep Mecca, and the Al Mutalib people
from killing our prophet, Mohammed?

And you, my cousin, reneged the deal in Al Medina,
Mohammed's time . . .

When will the day come?
When will you, Semite cousin of mine,
wake up and smell the jasmine
and put your hand in mine
so we can walk along River Jordan—
not me behind you
or you behind me . . .

Why can't we just talk—clear the air?
Why can't we live side by side,
and stop the bloodshed for crying out loud?
Who's wrong and who's right—
what difference does it make?
Can't we just share the Promised Land
So the world can rest in peace,
And leave us to have peace of mind?

And stop calling me Sand Niggah!
'Cause we both are—though you seem
to have forgotten . . .

I'm looking for some peace of mind.
I hope my Semite cousin is looking as well . . .
And please stop! Stop! Stop with the
'chosen thing' already—
it's getting really, really old.

How did it all start?
I wonder how it's gonna end . . .

SLEEP DEPRIVATION

Complications   multiplications
Pain never ending
Waves breaking over and over
Circular conversations
360 back to 0
Turning into 180
Byzantine arguments
Black-holed conversations

Husband said:
       "Excuse me, didn't we have this same
       Conversation for the thousandth time?"
Wife stated:
       "I don't know what the hell you're talking
       About, I thought you were talking about
       My own conversation"

We humans have our own perpendicular conversation
Like a cyclone   round and round
Like a little merry-go-round

Standing on a boardwalk   conversing with myself
Same conversation for the millionth time
Different boardwalks watching the waves
Breaking my thoughts   causing a chain reaction
In the wee hours of day break
Misery married to calamity   incongruent behavior
Same traffic whizzing by
Lost souls having what else   same conversations

What is it all about?
Confrontations and persuasions
Configurations that lead to disfigurations
Which reminds with the Mossad tactics
Of same conversations conducted in jail
With Palestinian political prisoners

Need to find me a new conversation
A new boardwalk
A new condemnation
Tired of past exploitation   and sleep deprivation

IN HELL (LEBANON)

Standing on a high mountain top,
Cadillac Mountain,
The highest on the northeastern seaboard,
Observing the Atlantic Ocean,
Huge rocks and trees surround me.
Waves conducting a musical symphony,
An everlasting view,
The mist running with the clouds,
As if they've been friends for eternity,
I felt that I'm in a strange heaven.

As my mind drifts away,
Thinking of my family, of my Lebanon.
I ran from the heat,
I ran from evil,
I ran from CNN and Fox News.
Last month sleep was impossible.
The world has gone to hell.
The enemy has no mercy.
The enemy is brutal.
The enemy is crushing and destroying
As though there is no tomorrow.

How long will this go on?
Buildings crumbling on children
And their mothers,
Bridges destroyed,
Houses demolished . . .
The enemy has no mercy.
The enemy is praying with a rabbi,
A hand of a mother
Covering her dead child . . .

The child is under rubble,
His blood pouring.
The child is crushed to death
In a Beirut building.
Beirut is destroyed.
What took fifteen years to build
Took thirty-four days to destroy.
Lebanon suffering again and again
Under destruction.

How long destruction will go on?
How long tyranny will last?
How long will the killings go on?

Sleep has departed from me.
In my waking moments
Feel like a never-ending nightmare.
My thoughts drifts
To my Nation, my Lebanon
Ya Qana   Marje'yoon   Bint Jbil   Khayyam!
Ya Haifa   Yaffa   Akka   Shaba'a!
Ya Beirut   Gaza   Jenin   Ramallah!

The enemy wants to wipeout Lebanon and Palestine;
The world is looking and not doing.
Where is Mr. Kofi Annan?
Where is Mr. Bush the Jack Ass?
Where is Condoleezza Rice the Whore?

I ask Allah
To have mercy on the Lebanese people,
To have mercy on the people of Palestine.
My tears run in the river of blood.
While I'm crying
On the children buried in the rubble,
On the mothers covering their dead children.

What did the child do?
What did the mothers?
What did Lebanon?
Do to the enemy . . .
Anger has infested,
Brutality is spreading,
The enemy has no mercy,
Prays then kills
Without a conscience,
Arrogant, pompous and brutal.

One day will come,
Righteousness will prevail,
And conquer misery,
Meanwhile the enemy is busy destroying.

My heart pounds for the children, Mothers &Lebanon.
I send my best to the fallen victims:
May they rest in peace,
As they absolutely did nothing.
And I salute Hassan Nassrallah
And Hezbollah
For standing up to the IDF army
For thirty-four days,
Unwavering, defending and dying for the land.

ICY LAKE

Driving into nowhere
Fogged up—Visibility   none
Passing Saratoga
The horses
Getting away from betrayal
Bickering and nasty e-mails
Grieving mother's passing
Fog   somewhat lifting
No end in sight
Entering a dead town
Lake George
Looking at the iced-up lake
Sheets and sheets of thick ice
Grounding the huge tour boats
Individuals crossing the lake on foot
Shuttered windows
Suddenly
A crisp rainbow shows up
A second one right behind
Orange—green—blue and double-purple
Drilling holes
Ice fishing
No fish to catch
God's creation in motion
Trees lined up guarding the lake
Naked   like an army guarding
St. Petersburg in Akhmatova's siege in 1941
White and green houses dotting the outskirts
Me howling like a wolf
Drinking Vodka to numb the cold and the pain
Tops of mountains with icy frosting

Adirondacks
Drops of gentle rain dropping on my head
Mixed with blood pouring from my hand
Little holes everywhere
Fear of sinking in the ice
Sticks in the head . . .

NOT YOUR DOG

Dear cousin Moshe
You keep shoving the so
Called peace down my throat
Insisting I should sign that note
Five wars—2 Intifada's and now Gaza
You want me to disappear from the Earth
You want me to rat on Hamas
You want me to be a dog like Abbas
To kneel on demand
To shit on command
What kind a peace is that?
My blood is reaching the knee
The other knee is blown out
My boat is stuck in the sand
You even kill the fish
That I need to eat
To make sure you slim me down

YO MOSHE,
When are you ever going to stop?
You and I should go back in time
The Cane & Able time
But for now Moshe
Blow up my home
Burn my skin
Cut off my limbs
Keep me a prisoner in my land
Keep throwing stones on my roof
I will never love you back
And as far as Cane and Able goes

I guess we are all going back
But for now Mr. Chosen Moshe
The souls of Gaza-Shatila and Deir Yassin
Will forever hunt you down . . .
I mean haunt you down . . .

Gaza under siege for the third year, March, 2010

IN A BETHLEHEM TOWN

Had a job in a distant time in a West Bank, Bethlehem town,
In an orphan land, hands clinging to mine, hard to let go, in a mission land.
Crossing checkpoints, no one cares; no one's lending a hand . . .
Watching their movements, running, craving for attention,
Staring dark eyes, beautiful young faces, *left behind!*
From atrocities of war, *left behind!* From refugee camps, *left behind!*
I wish I could adopt a child—not allowed in this brutal culture of Crazy Land,
Tears fall down when I turn around—*what to do? What to do?*
All I did was to spend more time playing soccer and basketball
To sing-along songs of childhood.
All the orphans are sons of mine—gorgeous eyes, olive skin, jet-black hair,
Children begging,

> *Please take me home! I promise, I'll be on my best behavior,*
> *I want to be loved, I need a real home, and I am tired of my cold dreary room.*
> *Pack me in your suitcase, I need a real dad, I need a real mom.*
> *Take me and never leave me behind, everyone leaves me at the end of the day,*
> *Left behind to talk to the walls.*

No warmth, no heat. Relatives visiting, not nice at all, watching *Ahmad & Amenah,*

Crying their lungs out.

In a land that has no mercy—adoption is taboo—no love, just war left behind.

Twenty years later, went back to adopt—*No sir, Muslim law doesn't allow, (only family members),*

Who don't give a damn?

> *I need your touch, I need your gentle smile, and I miss my mother that perished in the war. Please take me with you.*

Life is a journey, and my thoughts light the path . . .

In this hell-hole, out of all places, where is Jesus to save me in his birth town?
Where is Mohammad, prophet of mine?

> *I am all alone, I need some loving, I need to love you back, and I promise I will be good*

(always trying to console the children).

Intifada erupted, unable to get to work, missing the orphans and the good times, missing their cries.

Had to quit the job and get out of town—too much to bear.

In a Bethlehem Town, wonder if Jesus is still there to save the orphans left behind.

After all, it was his birthplace.

LAILA'S DEPARTURE (THE FINAL TRIP)

Jerusalem, February 5, 2008

Mother O Mother
You raised me
You gave me
You planted the seed of love in me
You gave the world all you got

Mother O mother
Hope you're resting in
A safe   beautiful   peaceful place
Mother I am yearning for you
Missing your laughter
Missing your gentle kisses on my neck
Missing your warm hugs
Missing feeling safe in your presence

The Bushkill waterfall misses you
The birds are singing for you
They land on my knee to console me
The valley of Jericho sends its best wishes

Jerusalem and Al-Sala'ah Bedouin town
The Negev Desert and the Dead Sea
The mountains send their breeze to you
The fog is lifting
The rainbow is here
Your departure is hard
I miss you
You will live in me

Farid S. Bitar

Missing your painting
Missing you lecturing me
The screaming is gone
Pain is finally gone

I love you mother
Till the next time we meet

MOTHER TERESA,

An encounter

Peaceful intonations
The complexity of the human
Demands of an apology
Complications on the 4th of July

Walking in Ocean Grove
Waiting in anticipation
Of a looming danger
Or not

Who walks right by me
But five of mother Teresa's nuns
Dressed in White & Blue
After they passed me by
I felt the urge to follow
I intruded on their space
And stated

Would you be kind to do me a favor?
The tallest one replied,
Which prayer you want performed?
What is troubling you son?

I was taken a bit & proceeded
Would you please pray
For the souls of Gaza-Jenin & Ramallah people
Behind the electric fence
Behind the wall
That Israel is insisting to erect
Pray for the starving—malnutrition children
        For the poor souls perishing in the desert.

They all replied at once," your wish will be delivered, actually as we speak,
Many of our sisters are in Gaza land, standing hand in hand with your
people, facing the monster".
And then they were gone.

Minuets later, they came back
One saw me wiping my tears
And insisted to know my name
I stated "No Name, I have no name,
just a Palestinian soul wondering
In the God bless America on the 4th of July"

Another said "we just want to pray for your peace of mind"
I declined the offer and insisted,
Please do not forget to pray and ask:
To put some sense in Goliath's head
To stop the killings and demolishing houses
To stop the vigilante style assassinations
Of leaders of the struggle for a homeland,
And let the food & medicine supplies be delivered to the needy and the
hungry in Abraham's land.

MAN-HANDLED ...

Go back   Go back
Traveling on the Commuter Jersey Line
Go back   Go back
Sonny just Go back
To the war raging
In Gaza land—In Jenin
To the grave yards of
Sabra & Shatila—Deir Yassin
Go Back   Go back
Where home is—Was and Will
Got Bunt headed by a commuter
Pushed the Adam away
He took me down—Karate style
Landed on the seats
Blood pouring from my arm
He yelled—stay down stay down
Stumped on my chest to keep me down
Sprung back up
I am not a dog to stay down
Got some more beating
While I was fighting back
Car emptied out
No one to lend a hand
Four cops barging in
Both of you come on out
Fuzz are scum, they barked
"You deserve what you got".

I'd rather go back
To the war raging land
Where I belong
Where safety is
Where warmth is plenty
Than to be Manhandled
      Mishandled
         Mistreated
And abused on the tranquil Jersey line . . . 8/13/09 attacked on the
Path . . .   By a civilian who was a black belt expert

SHOW ME THE WAY

No more tears

        No more fears

No end in sight

        Tunnel black

                No sign of light

World spins round and round

        Like a rolling stone

                Cruising on the ground

I get no satisfaction

        Mick Jagger said

Show me a way

        Show me a better way

                And let me

Go away

TALKING TO A MESSIAH (OF A KIND)

I approached the man and asked,
Who are you to be?

Are you the Son of God?
Are you Buddha, the silent observer?
Are you Ba'ahai, at the Mount of Carmel?
Are you the Second Coming?
Are you the sand niggah from the land of milk and honey,
Mohammad, Abraham, Moses, Jacob?
Are you the Real One coming back?

Please tell me, tell me,
Who are you to be?
I am lost—are you a mirage?
Figment of the imagination—are you an eternity in a day?

A glimpse of a new hope,
New World Order,
New ideas on the horizon
New revolution or No-It-U-Lover
Turned upside down.

To bring down a most evil Empire
And a sub-division of one in the Mid-East.
I still pay my taxes to finance killing Iraqi, Palestinian children.
Why do I obey blindly?
But I don't want to.
I live in a police state,
But I refuse to.

The price of oil is near five dollars—
Why on earth did we invade Iraq?
Why not sell our diamond rings
And feed Africa and Gaza land?
Dead are my people, it's enough.

Are you the enchanting *houri* (genie)?
Are you going to deliver us from this hell (Earth)?
Procession of mourners praying across from the U.N.
On the sixtieth anniversary of the *Nakbah* (disaster)
Praying for the dead still falling
Beyond the electric fence in Gaza
Beyond the wall in the West Bank
Beyond the walls of Basra and Baghdad.

It's a nightmare that never ends, keeps revisiting.
Intoxication, annihilation, and conspiracy.
Holocaust indignation
O! *houri* please make it go away!

Gibran said, "I felt like a prisoner, dragging his shackles
and impelled into an unknown place."

THE WALL

I want to talk to you about The Wall. The Barrier—Habinyan-al ha'it-al jidar. Not Pink Floyd's "The Wall" (my favorite group), not the famous China wall that stretches hundreds of miles. Not the Berlin wall, that came crashing down with the fall of the USSR. Not the Jerusalem wall, that stood form '48-67, and came crashing down in the six-day war when my father lost his first land and business. Not even the Wailing Wall, wall of the first temple adjacent to the Dome of the Rock—The Kotel—the holiest for Jews.

The Wall I want to talk to you about is the wall that I have been following since its inception in 2003. For the last three years Israel has been building this illegal wall to cordon the whole West Bank with the excuse of stopping suicide bombers.

By June 14, 2004 they reached Qulqilya and around Ramallah. By July 10, 2005 they reached the outskirts of my Jerusalem. Nowadays they are cutting four neighborhoods in Jerusalem, and cutting off almost 55,000 Palestinian residents. My sister's house is going to be on the other side; she is going to need a permit to go to work, her husband and her four boys, who go to school inside of The Wall, will need permits as well. It is going to take them hours to reach their destination; that is only one family of many thousands that are suffering.

Maybe the Israelis need a much larger wailing wall to cry over; this wall is nearing 800 miles and is not finished yet. They still haven't reached Bethlehem and Hebron, two holy cities for many. This Wall is driving me mad. It's cutting peoples lives. Orchards are cut in half. Daily living is interrupted because of this illegal wall. It's going around like a venomous snake, not even following the 1967 international border. In some places it eats five to ten miles into the West Bank to make sure it circles the precious illegal settlements, Ma'alee Adomim, Ariel, and many more. Settlements that are built on private Palestinian land. Even the Court Justice of The Hague handed down an advisory ruling that said building separation barrier inside the West Bank violated international law.

Thanks to Sharon, the father of the idea of settling in the West Bank, the number of settlers has swelled to more than 260,000. The settlements are so scattered, it's almost impossible to give back the whole West Bank. On top of that Israel annexed all of Jerusalem, and made it its capital.

"If The Wall is high,
> *the sky is higher still*
Close your eyes,
> *imagine you're an ant.*
The house will seem bigger".
> *From the movie Kandahar*

I toured the land in November 2003. What I saw was very sad. I call it the Swiss cheese theory: a checkpoint before you enter a town and a checkpoint before you leave, No Man's Land in the middle, only U.N. and Israeli army personal allowed.

I was there again for my father's passing in January 2006. The situation got a lot worse—The Wall had snaked to where my sister lives, Israeli Army apprehending Palestinians from the West Bank with orange documents. They just want to work and support their families.

Even Bush—the Hang Man—is getting jealous and wants to build a similar wall on the Mexican border, but not the Canadian one. The whole world, including the U.N. and all Arab nations, is opposed to this illegal wall.

I think this wall is a ploy by Israel to grab more land and to make things even harder so they can accuse the Palestinians when negotiations fail. I think this wall must come down. I think Israel should negotiate with the Palestinians on an equal basis and stop this madness of segregation and going back to the times of ghettos in Germany in the 1940's when the Jews lived like the Palestinians are living now. I think Israel has a complex, and they are never coming out of it.

TICKING BOMB
TICK-TUCK...
BOOM-TUCK...

Reflections on an airport day, Feb.8ᵗʰ, 2007

From 1:30 am till 6:35 am

Entering the Shrine of Ben Gurion Airport

Part I:
    Gaining permission of entry, 4 stops.
    1ˢᵗ stop, quarter mile away, half hour.
    2ⁿᵈ stop, before entering the actual doors of the terminals.
    3ʳᵈ stop, long line, X-rays, counter check, almost 3 hours.
    4ᵗʰ stop, in the back rooms, where no one sees, the actual humiliation
    and the interrogation, taking your clothes off, etc.

    Words: Passport check
    Who are you? 5 hours.
    Why do you come here?
    Palestinian/Israeli, Shin Beit/Mossad, missing the plane.

Part II:
    The Questions.
    Who are you?
    Why do you come here?
    Do you intend to come back and when?
    We told you not to come to our Promised Land . . .

    Words: New horizon
    Animal / Dirt
    Do not touch anything

Under the skin
Sweater, hat, glove.
Dog town: German Shepard. Doberman,
Fangs, Sorting / Weeding . . .

Part III:
Conclusion: Never come back to our Promise Land.
You also need more than 5 hours of misery & pain.
Words: Whose Promised Land?
Short fuse, humility, human touch?
Strip search, hands up,
Disgust, vomit, expectations.

Part IV:
The Human touch, or the lack of it.
The way we go about treating each other under the gun.
Dog town, fangs showing to lunge at the prey.

Palestinian and proud of it.
Tick-Tuck, Boom-Tuck, Ticking Bomb under my skin.

Words: under the gun, annihilation, deterioration,
Whose Promised Land?
Peace long gone.
War lingers for a very long time, I wonder why.

(performed on the Tablas)

ETERNITY AND A DAY

Ithaca has not deceived—
                Ithaca is rich and not poor

Besieged and liberty
                Idyllic day

Poetic haunting

Exiles in exile from
        Life—wife and dire straits

        How long does tomorrow last?

If I can only hold the moment
                So I can pin it on my chest
Like a Butterfly   Butterfly, you fly!

Korfula   my flower dies
                In the desert

Ella Ella Ray Ragamotos
                Pussty Ray

The wind takes your eyes
                Far away

I hear the footsteps
                Echoing in my house

Sobrecho Vassilis Khristos

Now I face the sea
                There is no end to it

Why have I lived my life in exile?
                Why must we rot in this life?

Help-less-ly

Or retrieve lost words from
                Silence

How long does tomorrow last?
                Argadini

It's very late

I stand here and
                Wait for you trembling

I wait for you by the sea

The Poet asked

How long does tomorrow last?

His lover said

An eternity and a day

Korfula   Korfula   Moo

I stand facing the sea
                Today is my day

Today is eternity and a day

HOMELAND...

You birthed me
    You gave me
        You suffocated me
            Yet, I still smell you . . .
In the Jasmine & Qurunful
In the streets of Gaza-Jenin-Nablus
Thirty years in exile
My umbilical cord
Still connected to you
I still dream of the casabas
I still dream of the Dome of the Rock
I still see the IDF soldiers
From my window
Breaking bones-Stealing
Killing civilians with their M-16's
My name is everywhere I travel
In every Airport
In every police station
I am famous all over town
I always ask:
What have I done?
To deserve all the notoriety
The whole world thinks
I am a destroyer
In actuality
I am a lover-misunderstood . . .

HOMELAND
>> Give me hope
>>> Give me sweet days again
>>>> Give me rivers of Banyass.

You told me,
You will come back one day,
You lied to me, you lied to me.
I am still waiting for you
I am tired of tick-tock . . . waiting-waiting
Ya Mawtinii . . . 3'ashiq-un—3'ashiqun . . .

I AM

Not the Son of Sam or Uncle Sam
I am the son of slavery and war
The son of misery and pain
Ghettos, projects left behind

  I am
Existing on the threshold
Razor-edged borders
Martin Luther King and Ghandi are my fathers
I still remember *I have a dream*
One day in Selma, Alabama

     His dream is being stabbed
     By the brutality of the NYPD
     Man gunned down
     Fifty bullets
     Newly-wed

     Amadou Dialo killed 'cause he was too dark
     African immigrant
     A gun was never found

     Visiting the projects is a hell of a time
     Bullets flying by the Bloods
     And the drugs
     Every time I'm there they think I'm from the fuzz

     Malcolm X (love the man—
     Saw the movie sixteen times)
     Nation of Islam shot the man
     Malcolm X is my main man

I am
Darfur Sudan
where the Janjaweeds are cleansing the land
Three million dead
Civil war for twenty years

I am
Rwanda
Hutu's and Tutsi's
Hacking each other machete-style
Eight hundred thousand heads falling down
Erected "The Museum of Skulls"
So they will never forget the genocide
Saw the movie *Hotel Rwanda* so many times
Cried time and time
   I am
Angola in the 70s and 80s
Civil war raging
Russians, Americans, Cubans involved
More than a million dead
When
When will it ever end?

I am
Nigeria, north and south
Muslim's and Christian's killing each other
The poor stealing the oil
Burning in the hundreds
Government corrupt—they sold their souls

I am
Algeria where the civil war raged
Muslim Brotherhood torching towns
Civilians dead in the thousands

I am
Somalia, Islamists retreating like rats
Civil war—Ethiopia involved
Another brother—imagine that

> Black Panthers almost annihilated
> Killed, jailed, exiled underground
> Resurrecting on the horizon nowadays
> Walking with Sharpton and Jackson
> Hand in hand
> Protesting fifty bullets
> Rule of law

> KKK still alive and well
> Still marching in the north and south
> Still calling African Americans
> Nigger this and nigger that

> That word is causing havoc
> The brothers use it as a term of endearment
> Whites use it as a term of disfigurement
> While I'm confused what to say or not say

I am
A civil servant HRA
New Yorker
My brothers are
Black, yellow, green—
Whatever is in-between

I am
HASA on the front line of misery and pain

I am
The Father of Soul, James Brown
I feel good . . . ha!

I am
Charles Rangel on the streets of Harlem

I am
Nelson Mandela, father of South Africa
Apartheid, man of Nobel peace, twenty-four years in jail

I am
Rosa Parks refusing to sit at the back of the bus
Honored in her death like a statesman should

I am
Rodney King and the riots of California
Riots of Crown Heights

But I am also
A dead civilian Palestinian
A dead Lebanese
A dead civilian Iraqi

I am
Martin Luther King, Malcolm X, a Black Panther,
Al Sharpton, Jesse Jackson, Andrew Young, David Dinkins

I am
The AIDS of Africa

I am
An African American and proud of it

>   No more slavery No more hatred
>   No more segregation
>   Prom night for blacks
>   Prom night for whites
>   Like in Augusta, Georgia
>   (Just saw a movie about that)

No more fifty bullets
No more Amadou Dialo
Just simply no more

Everyone is my brother
Why not honor MLK and revive his dream

And live all of us under a rising sun
In God Bless America

SKIN DEEP

While commuting on the morning train
I look into the horizon
I see the snow covering the fields and the rivers
Water ice cold
I remember days from many moons away
I remember my days in the University
They told me, that's I'm a bad student
I asked??? Why do you say such cruel things?
And why do you accuse me
That I'm no good
They told me, that the place
That I came from is no good.
So, for that reason
I must be, a no good person
I replied,
But my grades in Accounting, Economics and Physics are excellent
They said, you don't even know how to speak
The Language, but that's no matter
What matters, is that the blood
That runs in your veins is no good
They said, you're not welcome in this country
Go back to the war
Go back to destruction
Go back to your murdering people
The demolishers

The plane hijackers
The ones that kill innocent people
I said; I remember things quite the opposite
I remember, that my people were
Being killed in the refugee camps
I remember, the destroyed houses by the Zionist enemy
I remember, that my mother lost her mind and sanity

When her own mother, sister, nephew and my uncle
Perished in the war
I asked, why?
Why, do you accuse me of such cruel things?
I still remember, the fallen victims in
"SABRA AND SHATELA"
My aunt and her family were in Shatela
Thousands of victims, slaughtered like sheep
By the Phalanj—the Christian maronites
And then, a huge grave was dug for them
The whole world was watching,
No one was doing anything
I still remember the dark nights watching
NIGHTLINE—And SHARON was on the
Outskirts, watching and laughing
Why do you accuse me that I'm no good?
When the Zionists slaughtered my Nation
I still remember, Deir Yasin—
They wiped out 418 villages
The Urgun—Haganah—Stern gang
Menachim Begin was one of them
Why? Why? Why?
I'm pleading with God and asking
Him, to save my nation,
I pray that he will grant me my wish
I ask from God to free my nation
So we will live back in the glory days

1982-1983: The Israeli invasion into Lebanon. Sharon was the defense
minister and the moving factor to get rid of the PLO.

THE HUMANOIDS

A man standing in the middle of an aisle arguing
Holding the line in the car of the train
As if he only exists and only him
Lady behind him waiting so patiently
Uttering no words
The look on her face said it all

I remember the blue waters, nothing but blue
Oh my God, Hurricane Isabelle is coming soon
(I just finished watching the "White Squall"
Breath-taking but yet so horrifying)

My God, if we just learn to get along with each other
And treat others in a civil manner
Half the things we say we would never utter
We get so incensed and hurtful to each other

You are not my mother
You are just a woman who brought me to this world
I do not owe you a single thing
You do not exist
I come I go I do the hell as I please
Leave me alone do not bother me
Do not butt into my business

I am an independent individual
I do not need anybody
I can survive
I hate people
I cannot stand politicians
They are crooks
Let me breathe
Go to hell

THE JERUSALEM DRUM...

Born in a Holy Land
Born, I was born in
A land that knows
No peace
Old city
Where prophets walked
And memories burn . . .
Land of a thousand eyes
The never sleeps
And always weeps
In my veins
My childhood boy
Runs in the sand
Naked as a bird
Free in my soul
Above the Earth
Where the bombs explode . . .

Allah Ha'ie—Allah Ha'ie
Abdo Ha'ie—Abdo Ha'ie
Will-mali'ek (the owner)
Will-Kudoos (the sacred)
Wi-Salaam (the peaceful)
Will-Muha'i-men (the enforcer)

Allah Ha'ie Allah Ha'ie . . .

(performed on the Tablas . . .)

THE RIGHT OF RETURN

My luggage is packed
I always have my bags ready
Ready to go at any time
I have traveled for years
No destination, but one
Always complaining
No one is paying me any attention
No one wants to hear my story
Not even all the Arab World
They choose to ignore me
I landed in Cairo
To go to Gaza under siege
To visit my resisting nation
Mr. Mubarak said "no can do"
I mean Netanyahu and Obama
Changed his mind
My suitcase on my shoulder
In all of the airports
They call me a terrorist
They keep asking me to leave
And never come back
I always surprise them
By coming back

I don't care
I don't let it get to me
I never listen to anyone
I do what I want
One day will come
I will live in Jericho
Where it all started
And build that home

That I always dreamed of
And start my life
From scratch
After my death in exile
I demand from my land
To be created
So my soul can visit
Happily ever after
Instead of keep visiting
The land of Zion with lots of anger

Farid S. Bitar

THE EXILED

Four in the morning
My thoughts forbid me to rest
The suhur time (last meal to eat)
Ramadan is upon us,
Thinking of that terrible day
When I heard of Darwish's passing

Watching Darwish,
Tending to his garden
In Al-Barweh, his childhood village
Forbidden to enter since 48
Now his soul will dwell there
No need for visa's
No need for permission to enter
His soul will haunt its invaders
His poems transcending boarders
Lived in exile all his life
Beirut-Moscow-Tunis-Amman
Made love to Palestine from afar.

I think of Darwish,
The revolutionary,
The lover, the fighter
In exile, the enemy forbidding
His Burial in Al-Barweh

Was he also a dream?
He wrote and sacrificed
Eyes wide open, not shut
Apocalyptic horizon
Waiting for the sun
Crickets of the night
Moon-rising
The howling wolfs
The stillness of Lake Tiberius

I am a fool
I am a dreamer
Intoxicated in this wilderness

Darwish faced the enemy head on collision
Never ran away from his destiny
Luckily the Mussad did not assassinate him
So he can be:
         The voice of the tortured under the gun
         The voice of sacrifice & pain
         The voice of Palestine.

I am hoping one day
I will celebrate Eid-Al-Fiter with Darwish
In the garden of Al-Barweh.

Missing his words
Missing his face
All of Palestine misses you
My love to you is eternal
O! Darwish "where have you gone"?

I promise you, I will keep translating your poems
I promise you, I will carry on the struggle
I promise you, I will keep the voice of Palestine alive

Ramallah-Haifa-Jerusalem and Al-Barweh salutes you
I know your soul is dwelling in the land of Cana' an
Rest in peace, wa-rhamtulu llahu ala'ikaa wsalaam
I know I will hear you once more . . . In Al-Barweh when it's liberated.

Give birth to me again
Give birth to me again that I may know
In which land I will die,
In which land
      I will come to live again

                Mahmoud Darwish once said . . .

THE ISAIAH WALL

Running to catch the Newark subway line
Derailment   chaos   sardine time
Train jumped the tracks
Old lady sitting peacefully
Handing out a flyer
Heading: "Will there ever be a world without WAR?"
Now that caught my eye   I often ask that question
As I come form the land of Cana'an

      Have seen wars up-close and personal
      Have seen broken bones time and time
      Have seen bloodied humans in the Dehiesha Camp
      Splattered on the wall   red paint
      Waiting for the bull to charge in
      Have seen tanks open fire   no mercy
      And I still think I am in Jersey

Memories haunt me
Atrocities committed   never omitted
Checkpoints   strip search
Soldiers screaming   humiliating a civilian population

      At dawn walking in deserted streets
      Full of carnage and blood
      Walking along the River Jordan
      Full of hope and dreams
      Walking in the shadow of death
      Dragons spewing their heat

Memories of Hutus and Tutsis   machete style
Land of the skulls
Darfur Sudan going on and on
Cousin killing a cousin in Cana'an's land
Brother killing a brother in Gaza land
Serbs Croats Albanians holocaust style

>I keep hoping that one-day will come
>When tsunamis will end
>When earthquakes will end
>When the WARS will end

The Isaiah Wall at the United Nations:
>"They shall beat their swords into
>Plowshares. And their spears into
>Pruning hooks. Nation shall not lift
>Up sword against nation. Neither
>Shall they learn war any more"

One day will come
I will hold a white banner and stand
In front of the U.N. and demand
That there shall be NO MORE WARS

>So I can finally see green fields of wheat
>Growing trees in the forests
>Huge mountains with snowy tops
>See children not playing with cluster bombs
>But with dolls and peaceful toys

TUNNEL VISION

Standing in the last car
Staring into the dark star,
Muddy Waters,
Cars snaking through the tracks,
Tracks stretching, parallel lines,
Wooden slabs stacked like
A marching army.

Red lights, green lights, and in between,
The blinking orange light.
Neon lights passing one by one.
Side banks cushioning the cars,
Screeching halt,
Me slamming into walls.

White signs,
R—retreat, S—stop, P—proceed.
Electric cables, thousands of volts,
Conductor screaming,
14th Street, go to your job.

I lost my loved one, I trust no one.
Tunnel vision in the dark,
Oh, how I want to bark,
Intense conversation that led to annihilation.
Doom's Day is coming
And I feel that I am going.

VENGEANCE

Indemnity   brutality and pain
Opportunism and gossiping
Humans stabbing each other
In the back   in the front
Arms extended to be kidnapped
A messenger brought me news
I felt my life interrupted
I was listening this morning to a singer
Singing about love and vengeance
You are Beautiful
In punishment   in entanglement   in retribution
I see hands extended to the Human Race
I see stunning beauty
I see my life in the mist
I see God's beauty unmatched
I am frozen
My morals stuck in my bones
My state of mind has gone backward
And I'm reverting to vengeance

WHAT DO I TELL THE CHILDREN OF GAZA???

While the children are wasting away
While the children are malnourished
What I am going to tell the Gazan's
When I visit my homeland in December

Where should I visit?
The grave yards
The broken down places
The bloodied humans left behind
What do I tell the mothers & Fathers?
Who lost their entire families?
On the beaches—Harvested
In their homes,
While five girls playing with their toys
What do I tell the orphans?

Do I tell the Gazan's?
To rise up once more and fight
Or should I fight for them this time
They are exhausted from the wars
What do I say to them?
About the electric fence
Holding them hostage
Do I beg the Egyptian Government?
To let the Thousand Gaza March IN
And not to listen to Uncle Sam & Netanyahu

Please I beg of you to let us in
We want to stand with Gaza
To let them know they are not abandoned
I am coming with open arms
What do I pack to take with me?
Pencils—Notebooks—good paper
Heard the students have no supplies
Israel will not allow it
They do allow Pasta though

Words are not enough to console my brothers
My tears fall,
When I see the destruction
When I see the dead
When I see the injured

I keep hearing the cries of the children
In my dreams
In my waking hours
I am so frustrated
I am Fatoosh
The injured flying bird
Broken down on the Eretz crossing
Where is the conscience of the West?
And the Arab world

I wonder what Tel Aviv people are doing?
Are they busy sunbathing at the beaches?
I wonder what Haifa people are doing?
Are they busy with their café's?
I wonder what Jerusalem people are doing?
Are they deaf-mute & blind?
To the atrocities committed
Beyond the wall and the electric fence
Is the wall high enough for them?
Is the electric fence strong enough?

So Metula and the Negev desert
Will not hear the bombs raining down on Gaza
What do I tell Bi'lin?
While the IDF is conducting raids
In the middle of the night
Masked, so the world can't see their faces
While committing crimes of humanity
And threatening that
They will come back again and again . . .

Israel is claiming that
The Goldston report is unfair
They are only defending their land
They don't mean to kill innocent children
Its collateral damage
It's for the sake of security

When will Gaza rise from the ashes?
When is Enough—Enough?
When will the people of Gaza
Be able to go to the beach
Go to the parks and play
Go fishing
And live a dignified life
Just like their cousins—The chosen ones
On the other side of the electric fence . . .

WHY DON'T WE BREATH, COFFIN

To wreak havoc on this scrambled world
To flex muscles on Brussels
To get nasty with others
To Dominate
To maintain
To sustain
To Rule

We need to get nasty with each other
We poison anything comes our way
We go to the woods and the hoods
We come back with a clear head
We breathe carbon monoxide
We build more High Rises
We blast the mountains
We chop the jungles
We need H2O

We always want to demonstrate
We have to have the last say
We have to have cleaner air
We turn reality upside down
We go to the rain forest
We hate each other
We have a choice

Ice Melting
On the Polar Bear
Global warming creeping
Ozone layer—much too big
O! my dear Allah I know we can change . . .

UPROOTED TREES,

From my train window
I watch buildings going backward
In the reflection
The river is confused
I avoid looking into faces unknown to me
From my home window
I hear a large bang—five in the morning
Uprooted tree, falling on my neighbors house
What a scary sight
It could have been my bedroom window
The next day
Another huge tree
Decided to commit suicide as well
It's missing its sister
Shattering two brand new cars
My quiet street looks
Like a War Zone
Electricity gone for days
Food stinking the houses
No computer—T.V or I pod
Going back to simpler times
Takes me back to camping days
Nosey neighbors hanging out
I want to move out of this toxic town
To a house on a hill
Facing a lake
Glass all around
In no mans land
I want to go back to simpler times
My street looks like a scene from a GAZA TOWN . . .

TRANQUILITY

The gentle breeze
Is stroking my face
The birds are looming
In a violet horizon
Horses and feathers
Hamsters and suckers

I am a Sufi-dervish
Twirling, calling on
God's ninety-nine names
Soaring above the skies
Of Jerusalem and beyond
The Negev desert

I just want to soar
And reach the unknown
And break away from the shackles
I feel like a prisoner
In a body that does not
Belong to me
I just want to be free
From the entanglements
From the complications
That the human creates

I am still chanting God's names
In the searing desert of my ancestors
Drinking the blood of my invaders
On the Rock of Ascension

Farid S. Bitar

MA'ALIEH ADUMEEM (THE RED HILLS)

Ghostly faces
Death all around
Waving at me
While tending to mother
Her face
Between yearning
And a distant glare
Far away voices
Screaming in Hebrew
Do'daa Do'daa—Aifoo A'att

(Aunti—Aunti Where are you)
Another screaming voice
Fouling out obscenities
Cursing ghosts & 3izra'aeel
Thundering voices all around
Lapsing between eternity & obliteration
Enemy tortured in death

Ma'amma—Ma'amma—A'iekh a'att

(Mother—Mother where are you)
Mother also screaming
From haunting long term memories
She's calling her mother & sister's names
"They took an emergency exit
From the napalm bombs
Dropping on their heads in the war of '67"
They must be back for a visit
Not sure what's going on
Sister—sister
I am coming—make room

Standing in the middle of a large wing
Full of unpleasant odors
Faces expecting the angle of death
A man clearing his guts

That is the life we endure
Faces of our mothers and fathers
Writing about this grim reality
In one of my darkest days
In Ma'alee A'adumeem
In an Israeli settlement

Built on my stolen ancestral land
Where the enemy is taking care of mother
Observing her rather skeletal body
Her gibberish conversations
Her beauty far gone
I smile from pain
When mother attempts to curse
Cause in her waking hours
Hardly ever swore
She opens and shuts her eyes
And travels to another place

A lone star in a dark sky
A butterfly—fluttering
Lands on my knee
To bring me good news
I want to believe
It's the blue-star butterfly
From the valley of Jordan
Or is this butterfly
Is sent to lie to me
"Mother where have you gone
Why have you left this other creature behind."

MAKING LOVE IN AHMADIYA

You are my *askindenya*
Passion fruit of Jerusalem
Please have mercy on me

Let's fly to the south of Spain
Let's fly to the Himalayan plateau
Let's fly to Machu Picchu, Cuzco, Peru

Let's fly to another galaxy
And leave this troubled world behind
Let's fly to the Rock of Gibraltar
And have fulfilling conversations
Let's become gypsies in Andalusia
And compose poems of love

Let's sing and dance in a white space
With the whirling dervishes in Morocco
Let's elevate to a serene and tranquil place
And transcend to a new era unblemished
Let's fly on the wings of the clouds
And weave colorful rainbows

Under a magnificent waterfall Montmorency
Watching you wetting your upper lip
I want to hold you feel you
Breathe your *hawakii* (air)
Where the birds are chirping
And the sun is glaring

And we are making love
In Tikrit in Ramadi
Where Saddam's head fell
In Haditha (the massacre in 2005)
Where the Marines slaughtered fifteen civilians
In Ahmadiya Iraq The Sunni Triangle

Where the American soldiers
Are coming back in body bags

SELFISH BEHAVIOR

Life is a gift, we never asked
We love to live but time flies fast
Our life is designed for our satisfaction
We master it to perfection

We live to take as much as we can
We are taking lives   we are causing pain
We are eating the hearts of other people
We take a lot but return very little

A little slap   a little kiss
A little war   a little peace
A little love   a little hate
A little thought   for a big debate

This world is greedy   souls are dry
Our eyes are empty but we don't cry
We grab   we take   we use   we buy
It's a gift to live   we live to die

THE KISS

How I have longed for this . . .
The prelude to the kiss
How I have imagined it to be . . .
It was even more than I could bear
To kiss a goddess on this earth
Is like to kiss an angel
In the moving clouds

TRIAGE

a man selling poison
to poor souls coming out
from the gates of hell—HASA
approached the MAN
"stop doing that—it's a shame"
he replied, "you are disrespecting me"
"chased me away crossing the street
reported me to the devil Miss Jones"
Sgt. Miss Jones, tall, fat & ugly
her hair has seen better days
walks with a bulge worse than a man
lunged at me with her fangs
cooked a deal with deep throat
pocked me in the chest, spitting at me
calling me haunkie
I replied, I am olive skinned
put her hands on me to cuff and arrest me
they locked me up in Triage-Bellevue
released six hours later
Two doctors—two nurses and a social worker
Sir "we don't find any—ting insane about you,
you may go, with a nasty smile"
they stole my $200 dollars
they stole my pride and dignity
they treated me like a criminal
better yet, like they treat HASA clients
the shoe is on the other foot
It did not feel so good
wife looking for me for hours with no luck
while I was inside getting fucked
the hand that was dealt to me
was cruel, severe punishment

ordered by devilish deep throat
the lies she stitched, behind my back
the friendship she struck with devil Ms. Jones
two asses belong in hell
for days I don't sleep
fabrications—fabrications
indignation—criminal injustice
deceits—lies—human creation
dignity—Pride and honor
down the gutter
humans with black hearts
no compassion or mercy
I was lost in translation
I was brutalized—assaulted
confiscated in Triage
If all of Egypt rose
and cried enough to tyranny
I will also rise
I will demand my dignity
I will re-claim my sanity
Not that I ever lost it
18 years later as a case manager
I get a personal escort
ordered by deep throat
accompanied by the EMT & FD-NY
threatened by the FUZZ,

Human & a humbled soul, 2/04/2011 black friday.

THE LOSS OF INNOCENCE
International Activist...

She was born in the heart land of America,
She had the human touch, wanted justice to
The people that are so distant form her,
I believe she didn't know much about,
Till she journeyed to the Promised Land,
She was part of an international aid group,
Concerned about a nation under the gun,
Not a supporter of Hamas or the fundamentalists . . .

I wrote about Rachel Corrie in May of 2004,
A friend, invited me on Dec.16, 2006,
To the Minetta Lane Theater to see,
"My Name is Rachel Corrie",
Was not too sure if I wanted to attend, but I did.
It was about this couragefull woman who gave her
Life to my cause . . . My Nation . . .
Gave the ultimate sacrifice . . . her life . . .

Watching the crowd in the back of the theater,
Listening to what the script was all about,
The set full of rocks—bullet ridden walls—
The sound of gunfire, took me back to a dark time,
The voice of the actress going on & on . . .
Telling a horrifying detailed events,
Describing in depth the events leading
To that tragic day—March 16,2003—
When Rachel walked in front an Israeli bulldozer
To stop it from demolishing a house
Of a Palestinian family, her friend Dr. Samir's,
Her body visible to the driver of the monstrous machine,
Yet she was killed like an animal . . .

Killed for a cause that was not hers—
Killed for a cause that she wanted to help—
Killed for a cause to make a difference and stop—
To let the whole world listen and stop—
To just stop this madness—the atrocities that the
Israeli government was committing against a
Civilian population—unarmed—

Tears were falling like a heavy downpour,
Couldn't help myself, I was trembling—
I was so moved—I was so honored to be there—
To know that the pain of my Nation is being heard,
By the American public—
Now the shoe is on the other foot,
We will see what the outcome will be . . .

"My name is Rachel Corrie"—I salute you,
I will always pay my respects to you,
And your grieving family.

My name is a dead Palestinian civilian,
My name is a dead Lebanese civilian,
My name is a dead Afghan civilian,
My name is a dead Iraqi civilian . . .
My name is a Palestinian soul—
        Wondering in exile—no home to be found—
My name is pain and misery, never ending—
My name is Rachel Corrie, Palestinian refugee,
        Lost soul, wondering soul—
My name is Palestine—Darfur Sudan—Iraq—
        Afghanistan—Rwanda—Armenia—

My name is not RUMSFELD,
My name is not SHARON,
My name is not CHENEY,
My name is not BUSH . . .

My name is Tom Hurndall—Activist killed 4/11/2003,
My name is James Miller—Journalist killed 5/03/2003,
My name is unknown dead civilian killed by the thousands . . .

I waited to talk to the actress,
I chalked up but managed,
To finally thank her for getting the word out,
For telling the story of Rachel Corrie,
For telling the story of the civilian Palestinian misery & loss . . .

Rachel Corrie was in Gaza for a short period of time,
Paid dearly with her life to stop the madness,
I too was there for twenty years of my life.
I too witnessed a Jeep full of soldiers zooming
On a boy no more than 14 years old,
Beating the living daylight out of him,
Blood everywhere, his mother wailing hysterically,
Tearing her cloths, soldiers dragging the boy into the Jeep,
Me, trying to console the devastated mother.

I too was a witness to a busload full of Palestinian men,
From Beit Sahour, brought in to the orthopedic hospital,
That I used to work at in Bethlehem, they all had broken
Bones—legs—arms & ribs, inflected by the Israeli army.
They where all proud, I used to turn around and cry . . .

I too was there, when a soldier at a checkpoint—Herodze Gate—
Pointed an M-16 machine gun into my stomach and lifted the
Safety pin to shoot, my mother screaming at him,
that soldier was no more than 18 years old,
his commanding officer ordered him to
Stand down; my life this time around was spared . . .

I too witnessed a soldier beating the crap of a man ahead of me
At a checkpoint at—Hebron's Gate—, man bleeding profusely
From his head, I was next to the slaughter, told the other soldier
That I am a tourist, and that I am staying at a youth hostel in the old city,
soldier let me go, but I heard his footsteps behind me,
I knocked at that Hostel's door, pleading with the owner to
Let me in . . .

I too lost my grandmother—Um Munir—killed by a Napalm bomb,
I too lost my Aunt—Amineh—killed by the Israeli Army,
I too lost my cousin—Sa'id—killed by a bomb,
I too lost my uncle—Ma'rouf—killed by a shell . . .

In closing, I would like to ask for a moment of silence,
To honor the life of Rachel and the thousands of civilians
That fell with and still falling in Palestine—Iraq—Afghanistan—Sudan—
where the civilians are paying dearly with their life's.

ROOM WITH A VIEW (NOT REALLY), PART I

Just landed in New Orleans, 3:45 pm, March 22, 2005.
Insisted we hop on a city bus;
I like to rough it,
Wife moving along with a sigh,
"Don't believe in taxis? I guess not."
"No," I replied.
Wife: "Ummm," growling like a tiger . . .
Got to the first hotel, which was already
booked in advance by a time share.
They promised a four-star hotel;
they claimed "The Best of the Rest."
The name of the hotel was "The Cotton Exchange."
From the name of the hotel and being in New Orleans
I was thinking that I will be in the midst of
the Cotton Fields covered with amazing trees,
which is what New Orleans is famous for,
among other things: Jazz, the French Quarter, etc.
To our surprise the room wasn't just an average,
ordinary looking room, just like hundreds of
other hotel rooms that I already checked into.
Oh, wait just a minute, it was even more outstanding
than the other times:
bathroom door broken into halves, door
refused to shut.
Tub water clogged up, refusing
to go its merry way.
The best surprise is yet to come.
At last and to my total disappointment
I always like to open windows to check the outside view,
as I always ask for a quiet room with a view.
To my amazement I opened the shades:
a huge parking lot, six stories high, full
of disgusting autos, directly facing my room.

Now, that took all the fun out of my long trip.
Two airplanes, five hours, city bus, one hour.
Many attempts were made to change the room.
I was informed that half the rooms face
this magnificent parking lot.
I was told it was actually an historic parking lot.
With Love From New Orleans
I was so disappointed that my wife and I
decided to check into another three-star hotel.
Sleep Inn, in beautiful downtown N.O.
I specifically asked for you-know-what—
a "Room With A View"
and when we got to the room
the first thing I did was to open the windows
to check on the view.
I first looked upward; it was a foggy day,
pleasantly surprised.
I saw a stunning tall building top
lit in white: City Hall.
I yelled, "Eureka!"
But to my total disappointment,
when I looked down,
a huge parking lot was staring at me in the face,
with more disgusting cars waving at me,
"Hope you enjoy your room with a view."
With love, from New Orleans.

BARE BRANCHES

Standing in the middle of a cozy park
between the twilight of huge office buildings
somewhere in Brooklyn Heights,
admiring the bare branches of so many trees,

Small, lined up like an army battalion,
in full harmony, like standing guards in London Square,
unmoved by the wind, noise, hustle & bustle of onlookers,
unaware of their entwined, delicately shaped branches.

It reminds me of a trip I just came back from—New Orleans.
There in that garden district are huge, very old,
majestic trees, over touring the horizon.

Lined up in straight rows along Bourbon Street,
trolleys passing by loaded with tourists heading to the zoo.

Branches so long they cover the magnificent,
old New Orleans houses along Canal Street.

I was so taken by the dazzling scenery that
I missed my stop along with my wife.
Had to walk back a mile, back to the famous zoo.

Passing trees that are at least a hundred years old,
bark and roots of trees so thick—
they penetrate the asphalt, sidewalks and over towers,
the huge mansions . . .

I have never seen trees with such splendor, elegance and beauty.
Each tree has a personality of it's own.

I would love to name each tree
Peace   Splendor   Love   Tranquility   Magnificent

AH-WA'AKI

Ah-wa'aki   Like a circle around my heart,
Like a chestnut in the winter.

Ah-wa'aki   Please do not depart,
Promise me you will cling to life.

Ah-wa'aki   Like a burning coal in my heart,
Like a yearning soul for a start.

Ah-wa'aki   Your blood runs in my veins,
I think of you, all of the time.

Ah-wa'aki   *Ya silsalu qalbi*, for eternity,
Like a chain around my *corazon.*

Ah-wa'aki   Please do not leave me
To the dogs of this world.

Ah-wa'aki   I miss our eyes meeting,
I miss our meaningful conversations,
I miss your kisses on my lips.

Raise yourself form me
    And do not choke me.

Depart form me
    And do not have mercy on me.

ENIGMA—WHO AM I...

I spend my life digging in the sand
To build a hut that never stands
It keeps getting demolished
By the mighty chosen people
Who roamed the same sand
Forty years to be exact
Pay back is a bitch they say
It's my turn to live in the Diaspora
Netanyahu-Sharon & Begin say
My friends are the birds
I am a dream without a memory
I am a nation without a country
I am a country without a nation
No borders stop me
No family wants me
Broken down at the fence of Eertz
You always find me at the Police stations
I am a notion with no emotion
Waiting for Salah Al-Din to return
The right of return is forbidden
Soon enough it will be stricken
So I can finally go back to my beloved
Hope the Shin Beit & the Mossad
Are waiting for me in Ben-Gurion
As usual . . .
I am a Gazan child
I spread whatever love is left in me
My mother is Rafah
My father is Ariesh
My sister is Ramllah
My home is the CAMP

I am Destruction
I am a Lion with no teeth
I am a fire with no heat
I am a twister blowing in the wind
I am Haifa—Yaffa—Jericho

I carve my name in the dust
Hoping the birds will take my seed
Into the distant lands
Waiting for my resurrection
I am Sheikh Jarra'ah
Houses confiscated
Donated to the settlers
Demonstrating peacefully
Getting harassed & thrown shit on
By the settlers and the IDF
I am Imad Rizka
Getting shot in the head
With a gas canister
Donated by Uncle SAM
I am the streets of Ajami
In the heart of Jaffa
Still complaining since 48'
I suck the milk from the nipples
Of the refugee camps in
Dehaseha—Khan Yunis and Deir Ammar

I am a nation
I am memory
I am a lion with no teeth
I am a fire with no heat
I am the Revolution
I am the Revolution

Anna Gaza—Anna 3'issa
Anna Hulmun bila Zikra
Anna Sha'abun bila dawla
Anna Tiflun min A'afra
Anna Al-Thawra
Anna Al-Thawra
Anna Habbasun bila Asnan
Anna Na'arun Bila lahabun . . .

FROM MY TRAIN WINDOW

I see water moving in haste
An Egret worshiping on his own
Waves in the East river
Having a meeting of a sort
Maybe angry at the ships passing by

I see confiscated horizon
A brother stabbing a brother
After a favor was done in kindness
A man starring in the dark
Harvested civilians in Gaza
& the Mavi Marmara-Turkish boat
Pumped bullets in the chest
Of a Palestinian father in East Jerusalem
Four in the morning by a settler

Houses evacuated in a flash
To make room for settlers from Chicago
While the owners set up a tent outside
Settlers burning the Qur'an in Beit Fajjar
Scrolling graffiti in a Bethlehem mosque
Chaos all over the place
All that while commuting
On the peaceful Jersey line

GREEN EYES OF AISHAH,

roaming the streets of Gaza-Rafah
checking on a population under siege
I glimpse a stunning beauty with a Hijab
I chase her in the lobby
I chase her on the beach
swimming not allowed
don't care if Hamas is a guard
don't care about rules of engagement
don't care about the pointless meetings
Instead I'm gazing into her Green Eyes
deciding what shade of green they are

she's dangerous—you know
always gets what she wants
many times I said No—
she said please with her eyes
screamed at an Egyptian guard
for intruding on my Green Eyed Hurma (woman)
still wearing the Hijab

when the time comes to say
ma'a al-salaamah (good bye)
I could not turn my back
Insa'allahu we meet in Rafah
smuggled in a tunnel
under a white tent
so I can make love
to her green eyes
and find out what's under the Hijab . . .

Dedicated to Aishah with the Green killer eyes . . .

JOURNEY INTO THE ABYSS

Splattered limbs
On the rocks
Where the waves
Are making love
To the shores of Gaza
Knocking at the gates of HELL
Demanding with urgency to be let in
Pouring blood from gun shots
By high velocity bullets
By mercenaries on the high sea
In international waters no less
Bullets pumped into civilians
On the Mavi Marmara boat
From far away naval Israeli ships
From Apache helicopters
Landing on deck
With M-16's machine guns
They claim in self defense
Bodies falling down
Stunned faces in disbelief
Bullhorn blaring
Stop shooting, we come in peace
Gunfire kept coming from all around
Furkan Dogan, I feel your pain
I know you are coming back
I know you are busy preparing
Hundreds of Flotillas
With wings this time
Crossing the lines of scrimmage
Undetected by the IDF
So you can finish feeding
The civilians in Gaza

Exhausted from a 3 year blockade
Don't forget to bring Salah El-Din
He said he wants to return too
So do the other family members
So do the other 5 million exiled to Lost Island
Exiled by Netanyahu and Lieberman
To make sure this return business
Will never take place
Think again Mr. Urgun and Shitaret
This Flotilla is just the beginning
Of a great journey

LOUD BIRD AND A SHOE

Wake up cursing this damn bird
Wake up cluster-disturbed
This loud obnoxious singing bird
screeching his lungs out
worse than a siren

Calling to his mate
but she never comes
(I think he's horny—
didn't get his fix the night before)

Hiding in a huge tree
over my boring house
bird on a string
I can never find
I have a shoe to throw at him
Looked for him for an hour
to no avail

Inconspicuous
Singing a sad song
What am I doing
With this mixed-up logic
shoe in hand?

Where has my mother gone?
She was where pain dwelled
I keep searching for answers
Does Doom's Day exist
or is it just a myth to deceive
fools to do good
build blocks for an afterlife?
I think the final chapter is dust
swirling in another galaxy

I finally find that loud bird
Red cardinal looking for
his yellow mate
Where has my father gone?
Is he with my mother Laila?

I'm running to work like
a Pavlovian dog!
Swiping that miserable clock
one day my heart is going to give out
from running to catch the time
before it's too late.
Monday is a Wednesday
and I will have for lunch on Friday
what I had for dinner on Tuesday
Office days are all the same
different times same faces
But that bird is always singing
His days are more interesting
His scenery is awesome
My days are not
Bird on a string
I have a shoe to drop

STOP SIGN

Judge   Jury   Executioner
At midnight got a ticket
Running a stop sign
In a sleepy town   everyone dead
No motion   no traffic   no commotion
Rookie cop
Nasty demeanor
Slapped me a fine
Came back with another
Barking dog   threatened me
With a bench warrant
Had to comply

First time around   waited three hours
Cop never to be found
Second time around   brought in a witness
To prove my innocence
Cop lying   insisting that I never stopped
Drawing an erroneous map
Judge irritated   guilty as charged
Doubled my fine   screamed at me
To get the hell out of his court
Felt like an animal
Being thrown into the slaughter
Hate this town with a passion

Third time around,
Waited to the last person,
To be seen,
Judge—remembered my face—
Yelled at me form the top of his lungs,
Go pay your stinking fine,
And get the fuck out of this town,
Felt—ejected—dejected—contradicted
No respect—No one to ask for help,
Escorted by the officer of the court
Told to pay my fine.

I am not a criminal to be treated as such
I pay thousands of dollars in taxes
And the thanks I get
They want to arrest me because I insist
That I am innocent

God Bless America
The land of laws and dejection
Racial profiling
Running amok
Judge that can't stand
The Arabs in his town
They want me to get out of town
Just because my name is a threat

THE VISITOR...

O! Standing erect
I am sad
In my Diaspora
I am sad
In my celebrations
I am sad

O! Flaming apparition
Pour me a drink of blood
I am thirsty
O! Visitor
What is your request?
Is it to enter or leave!!!

Give me peace,
Peace of strength
Not weakness
Are you asking about my well being?

Give me serenity
O! Dear one
Asking about the universe or what?
Why do you come to my dreams?

O! Father   O! Father
How are you?
Do you come to ask about my mother?
And can I see you again?

THE WHITE MAJESTIC EGGRET

In anticipation of the time
when the train snakes through
the bodies of water in between
Newark, Hoboken, I get full of hope—
positive thinking—
as I am about to find
that majestic white, long-legged
bird, perched on the water.
Oh . . . I see one hiding in the tall grass
So breathtaking
full of radiance, elegance
I see another one standing on a small rock
in the middle of the wetlands
Behind him in the distance
a highway bridge that is crossing over
connecting civilization to various destinations
The bird standing on the rock, no movement.
unaware of what the world is running for
Spreads of ongoing green lands of tall grass
blending with bridges, highways
In the middle of it, small rocks popping up
like small islands
There is where the King of the Wetlands
stands like a proud ruler
protecting its boundaries from
invaders of ducks, geese, and seagulls
He declares his kingdom
stands there all alone
paying attention to no one
as if he's in a deep meditation
transcending to a different plateau
I hope that one day I can disembark from

the train between the stops to say hello
to the White King of the Wetlands
and thank him
for putting a smile on my face
I am a great admirer of that bird
I always look out for that crane
We have this connection from great distance . . .
Other birds stand together, line up
Ducks march in a straight line
one family at a time, couples
Seagulls fly in a group
but not this white crane
He is all on his own
He is the King of the Wetlands

WHAT'S THE POINT

Standing in anticipation next to a train window overlooking the horizon,
  Heading to Hell (The Job).

Glaring, in a conspicuous daze, thinking, What is the point?!

Huge, tall glass buildings, rivers running in a quiver.

Dust. Climax. Extreme makeover.

Woman in Jordan strapping a suicide belt that's set to go off in the middle
  Of a wedding.

Oh, wait . . . it failed to detonate. Later Sajida's caught in an empty room;
  How it happened so quickly is amazing.

(Though her husband succeeded and took tens of lives.)

Blue skies. Muddy waters. Sunny clouds.

What a day. I guess Saddam will never go away.

Another day just ended, another day just started . . .

Took the same train again; it's been five years of the *sameagain.*

See the same usual suspects, over and over, all of the aspects . . .

What is the point?

We go on with our daily grind; I hate the crowds, the shoving
  In the sardine time.

Another weekend, another weekday, it's all the same . . .

All days just look alike—if I don't have a watch or a calendar
   I'm sure it's all the same . . .

Trucks rolling, cars whizzing by.

Tornado's. Cyclone's. Devastation.

Suicide bombers ending it all . . . What does it mean? Where are we heading?

It's all the same—suicide belts.
London. Gaza. Baghdad. Amman. Madrid. Jerusalem. Riyadh.

What's the point?

We humans appear, destroy, and disappear
   Leaving not much of a trace.

Whether we're famous or an average Joe, we all go
   Just the same, six feet under.

What is the name of the game? So, what is the point?

I beg you to tell me, what the hell is the point
   Of this game, if it's all the same.

On 11/9/2005 three hotels in Jordan were bombed, leaving 57 dead and 110 injured. In the Middle East the date is written with day first, then month; thus: 9/11/05.

THE VIOLIN MAN

I was taking time out
almost ten minutes passed
I just didn't want to leave
I was the only one standing
and listening
I guess I had to move on
you know   worshiping the dollar
the job
that's waiting on the horizon
I couldn't help myself
I had to approach
The Violin Man
As hard as I resisted
I couldn't help but to tell
the violin man that he put
a dent into my rather
dull routine day
So I said *Thank you Mr. Violin Man*
Thank you from the depths of my heart
Thank you for giving me hope
The Violin Man was playing
from his insides out
My favorite classical piece
of all time
Vivaldi's *The Four Seasons*
He was consoling me
he was crying with me
He was absolutely
Superb
His violin was full of passion
joy   sadness   madness

all at once
This is what I call time out
from the madness of
New York City
People running to nowhere
People running after the Green God
This city is driving me
Mad as hell
Thank god for
The Violin Man

BURNING

Feeling lost   feeling confused
Eyes will not shut down
Burning and deception
Retribution and contribution
Feeling like a failure
My eyes observe everything.
I get angry at times
My sadness and tears . . .

I think and think   my mind can't turn-off
People abusing each other
They suck the blood   they never look back

Why do I do what I do?
Why am I here in this cyclone?
Why will not my end come?
So a new beginning can start
A happy-strange-mysterious beginning

I am tired
I want to shut my eyes
I want to open my eyes
Into a white light
Far away   in a distant land
I want to fly to another world
Where I only see blue and white
No more red

Depression is tremendous
It destroys lives
I just visited Abu Amar's grave in Ramallah.
The weather was stormy and rainy

I think of my beloved mother
I think of her well-being
I think of her thoughts, tears, and aspirations
In these difficult days
She's on shutdown

I always want to call her
To hear her sweet voice
I always hesitate
I wouldn't know what to say
I am longing for my mother
For my father   may god rest his soul
I am longing for my Jerusalem
For my Palestine

BEDOUIN BEAUTY

Dark but not stirred
Over my tears
The world is fluttering
Over the dead
I complain to you
I cry from my pain
I am stinking drunk
I am chocking on my
Bloody tears
I bitch to myself
About the status of the Universe
But no one listens
Not Netanyahu
Not Mubarak
Not Obama
Not even my therapist
But Osama, that's a different case,

O! Dark beauty of the desert
My eyelids are blinking
Twitching-fluttering
Over the dead in Gaza and beyond
Over the Iraqi civilians
They call them collateral damage
I hate that term
It' insulting to the human
My Qis-ma'atee (fate)
My Sudfa'atee (chances)
I cry to you my Samra'atee (dark beauty)
You just keep starring at me
With your killer Bedouin black eyes
And you never listen to me.

ABOUT THE AUTHOR:

Farid S. Bitar, born in Jerusalem-Palestine in 1961, schooled in the British and French systems, earned a BBA degree from CUNY-Baruch College in 1983, New York City.

Working as a social worker in the field of AIDS for the past 19 years, have been writing-editing and performing poetry with Tablas and Harmonica.

Edited a book of poetry " Treasury of Arabic Love" in 1997, produced a CD-Fatoosh in 2007, that narrates a personal story and a nation under occupation, produced a second CD-Shutat in 2009, also an activist in the field of politics, hoping that justice and a dignified solution with Israel will be at hand.